Hypatia of Alexandria

By Laurel A. Rockefeller

Cover art by Rachel Bostwick

This book is based on events in the life of Hypatia of Alexandria and constructed using primary and secondary historical sources, commentary, and research. Except when quoting primary sources, dialogue and certain events were constructed and/or reconstructed for dramatization purposes according to the best available research data.Consulted sources appear at the end of this book. Interpretation of source material is at the author's discretion and utilized within the scope of the author's imagination, including names, events, and historical details.

Explore these related biographies from the Legendary Women of World History Series

Boudicca, Britain's Queen of the Iceni

Cleopatra VII: Egypt's Last Pharaoh

Published by Laurel A. Rockefeller Books.

Johnstown, Pennsylvania. USA

ISBN: 197633280X

ISBN-13: 978-1976332807

Table of Contents

Prologue

"Magistra, the books you wished to borrow have arrived!" knelt the young novice as her prioress tended a patient at Disibodenberg in Naheland in west-central Germany.

Prioress Hildegarde rose and wiped her hands on a towel, "Excellent. Did the brother specify how long I may borrow them?"

"No, Magistra."

Hildegarde headed towards the priory library, "Well then I will have to ask him myself before he departs."

"May I ask—what is so important about these particular books?"

"They are the writings of ancient Greek mathematicians and astronomers. Wisdom of the ancient world, a world that was very different from the one we live in today," answered Hildegarde.

"But such knowledge is forbidden!"

"Yes, it is."

"Then why risk it?"

"God speaks to many people—not only to Christians. If there is something of value to be learned then I wish to learn it, no matter who God teaches it to." Arriving at the library, Hildegarde smiled at the table covered with over a dozen heavy volumes, "Thank you for bringing these, Brother. How long will your master permit me to review them?"

The brother picked up one volume, "Two months, though he said he would consider longer if the need should arise. He said you would be particularly interested in this one."

"'Nicene and Post-Nicene Fathers' by Socrates of Constantinople?'"

The monk flipped to the first page of chapter fifteen, "Yes. Take a look *here*!"

Hildegarde read aloud, "'Of Hypatia the Female Philosopher. There was a woman at Alexandria named Hypatia, daughter of the philosopher Theon, who made such attainments in literature and science, as to far surpass all the philosophers of her own time.' Intriguing! Do many know of this Hypatia?"

"No, Magistra."

"Because she was a woman?"

"I think perhaps the answer will become clear with further reading."

"Agreed!" smiled Hildegarde as she sat down and began to read.

Chapter One

Alexander the Great's masterpiece metropolis, the great city of Alexandria glittered like a jewel against the sparkling Nile River. Ships laden with exotic goods glided into its many docks as merchants readied for trading. Shop keepers watched anxiously for deliveries in the early morning light. The sound of heavy carts merged with the din of a thousand conversations in Greek, Latin, and Hebrew slowly grew louder. The rosy-fingered dawn yielded to a golden-blue day. In the main library Theon of Alexandria busied himself with returning books to their proper places. A middle-aged man approached him. Theon bowed to him respectfully, "Kaleemera keerie katheegeeta."

"Kaleemera, Theon. You are here early," observed the librarian.

"My wife is due to give birth anytime now."

"Then you should be at home, not here shelving books like a first-year novice."

"I am anxious for the birth and for her safety."

"All the more reason to be home."

"But what can I do? Would Eileithyia hear my prayers if I offered them? Surely not—that's if she exists at all."

"We can only do what we can do, Theon. Right now, your wife needs you more than I do. Go home. I promise the library will still be here when you are ready to return," smiled the librarian.

Theon nodded, "Efcharistó, katheegeeta."

Twenty minutes later Theon arrived home. A baby cried softly. Theon opened the door to his bed chamber to find his wife tired but safe, her new-born resting against her breast. The midwife turned to Theon, "Congratulations, Sir. It's girl."

Theon sighed with relief and thanksgiving, "Efcharistó, Eileithyia. Praise be to Eileithyia; praise be to Hera!"

Theon's wife smiled, "What shall we call her, Theon?"

"Hypatia for she shall be the greatest of all women."

"It's hopeless!" cried Hypatia as she threw her drop spindle across the room, her wildly uneven yarn unwinding clumsily from the spindle's shaft. Her nanny, a slave named Iola, picked up the spindle from the floor. Hypatia fell into her arms. "I can't do it!"

Iola soothed her, "My lady you are only five years old! Do you really expect yourself to spin as if you were a woman grown with children of her own?"

"Every time I try to draw the wool out it falls apart. When I try to mend the two ends together, it falls apart more."

Iola picked up the spindle and the wool and then sat in a nearby chair, "You can do it, I know you can. Here, watch, see how I overlap the two ends and hold both together between my fingers? Now hold that tight while winding the spindle tight and slipping it here into the notch and there into the small hook. Do you see?"

Hypatia sat down beside her, "Yes."

"Okay now watch as I twirl the shaft. The wool between my fingers is now tight and bound together. What I do next is slowing move my hand towards the part that is not twisted at all, not very far, just an inch at first, very slowly. See? Now here I'm going to wind the spindle so that the part we just put together is between the hook and the shaft. As long as this is tight, the yarn will not come apart and I can slowly start to draw it out again. See? It's not hopeless. You can do it if you practice," smiled Iola as she handed the spindle back to Hypatia.

Hypatia twirled the spindle. Out of control it landed on the floor with a soft thud, "I told you! I'm hopeless!"

"Hopeless at what?" asked Theon as he entered the room.

"Spinning! Patéras, I can't do it! I'm no good at women's work. I can't spin. I can't embroider. I can't sew. I can't cook! No one will ever want to marry me, at least not for my own sake!"

Theon sat down beside her, "With a good match you won't have to. Slaves will do it for you and you can spend your days doing whatever you wish to do."

"But what am I suited for, Patéras? How can I ever be a respectable lady like mother is?"

Theon smiled reassuringly, "Perhaps there is more than one way to become a respectable lady."

"How?"

"You could always help me with my work," offered Theon.

"A female philosopher? People will laugh at me—or worse! Zeus made Pandora, mother of all women, to punish mankind for the trick Prometheus played on him. There is no honour in being a girl and no place among the educated for girls or women to learn let alone teach as you do," protested Hypatia.

"The law commands that you, my daughter, obey me. Do you agree?"

"Yes. What do you wish me to do?"

"I command that you spend your days in study and when you are old enough, you will come with me to the temple where I teach my students."

"They will stone me if I come!" objected Hypatia.

"No, they won't, Hypatia, because I command it and under the law, you are my legal property. I have the right to take you to my classes if I wish and ask of you anything I desire. Not one man will act against it, no matter how he feels about your presence there."

"Very well then, Patéras. I shall obey. When do you want me to start?"

"Tonight. We will go up together to the roof to look at the stars and I will show you the geometry of the heavens."

Hypatia hugged him, "Efcharistó, Patéras!"

"You are very welcome, Hypatia!"

Chapter Two

One year later Hypatia sat at a small wooden table. Carefully copying letters from a baked clay tablet, she etched practice lines of each letter into the wax sheet in front of her. Theon bent over her shoulder, "Excellent, except your lower case xi ξ and zêta ζ need work. Here, let me show you." Picking up a second tablet and stylus from the table, Theon slowly transcribed the two characters in front of her. Hypatia copied her father. Theon smiled with approval, "Much better. Practice those until it fills up your tablet. After dinner, I will bring you up to the roof for more lessons."

Hypatia followed her father up the stairs to the roof, grateful for her heavy woollen palla which warmed her against the autumn night chill. Above them the stars wheeled majestically. Hypatia smiled at the beauty of the sky. Theon stepped to a small table and picked up his cross staff. Turning to the north he put the cross staff up to his cheek and measured the angular distance between Polaris in Ursa Minor and Alpha Ursae Majoris in Ursa Major.

Hypatia walked up to him, "What are you doing?"

"Measuring the distance between the pole star and that bright star near it."

"May I try?"

Theon lowered his cross staff and handed it to Hypatia, "That star is called Alpha Ursae Majoris. It's part of a constellation called Ursa Major –the big bear. Callisto was a beautiful nymph sworn to Artemis. One day, Zeus fell in love with her and she conceived a son. Hera of course was very angry that her husband had cheated on her again and turned her into a bear. One day her son, a young man named Arcas, met her in the forest. Naturally he was afraid that she would kill him—as bears often do when humans get too close. So, Zeus intervened and put them both in the sky. The mother is the great bear Ursa Major and the son is the little bear Ursa Minor. Callisto's body is formed by many stars, Alpha Ursae Majoris being the closest to Arcas' tail. If you will look here, the tip of that tail is the current pole star, Polaris."

Hypatia smiled, "It's beautiful! Why do you say 'current' pole star?"

"Because Polaris is not always the pole star. Sometimes it is Alpha Lyrae. About six hundred years ago, Hipparchus of Nicaea discovered, almost by accident, that the spin of the Earth is imperfect. Like a top, it wobbles so that the pole star alternates between Polaris and Alpha Lyrae. It takes a very long time, of course. The wobble is very slight – about one degree every seventy-two years. So as far as we need to be concerned Polaris is the pole star—and will continue to be for a very long time."

"So, if I want to find north, all I need to do is look for Alpha Ursae Majoris and I will quickly find Polaris?"

"Yes. It is as easy as that—at least at night it is."

"This is amazing, Father! I had no idea there was so much to learn about the stars!"

"The discoveries have only begun, Hypatia. Perhaps you will make discoveries that will change the world."

"I would like that very much! To learn all about the stars, all the secrets of the heavens and the earth. Will the gods reward me or punish me if I make this my life's work?"

"That is a question you must answer for yourself. But I think this is the path for you, Hypatia, if you want it badly enough."

"What must I do?"

"Right now, you must go to bed. I have kept you up far too long. When you are older we can spend more time studying the sky. Go to sleep. In the morning, we will work on your reading and I will teach you some basic mathematics that you will need to understand before you can study the stars."

Springtime came to Alexandria. Leo and Cancer wheeled high into the night sky. In the northwest corner of the city Jews prepared for Passover by cleaning out every grain of chametz from their homes and businesses. Rabbis watched over the preparation and baking of matzo; early flowers began to bloom in public gardens. Memories of the cold winter's chill faded away; the entire city blossomed.

Humans too blossomed. Now ten years old Hypatia was quickly growing into a beautiful and confident girl on the edge of womanhood. Strolling through the gardens Hypatia noticed a Jewish girl sitting alone. "Salve mi amica mea, quomodo es!" smiled Hypatia.

The girl stood up, "Salve!"

"It's a beautiful morning," remarked Hypatia.

"It would be more beautiful if Passover were over," replied the girl. "I'm sorry, I shouldn't complain. My father is a cantor at our synagogue and my parents are very religious. My name is Rachel bat Levi."

"Pleased to meet you Rachel. I am Hypatia, daughter of Theon."

"The mathematician and librarian, that Theon?"

"You've heard of him?"

"Yes, of course. In my culture books are very important, the Torah most of all."

"I cannot say I know much about Jewish culture or religion. My father has me busy reading all the great Greek and Roman writers, particularly the philosophers."

"I would love to study the Torah, but is it proper for a girl? There are no women rabbis."

"But surely learning for its own sake is valuable!"

"Learning for men, certainly! My brothers often are found studying the Torah. But the propriety for women and the Torah is hotly debated. Some of our leaders feel Torah study helps women overcome our natural moral deficits. Others feel that our natural inferiority makes Torah study inappropriate. For how can a woman ever understand the words of G-d as taught in the scriptures?" asked Rachel humbly.

"Aristotle said,'… the male is by nature superior and the female inferior, the male ruler and the female subject. And the same must also necessarily apply in the case of mankind as a whole; therefore, all men that differ as widely as the soul does from the body and the human being from the lower animal these are by nature slaves, for whom to be governed by this kind of authority is advantageous, inasmuch as it is advantageous to the subject things already mentioned,'" quoted Hypatia.

"Are you Greek or do you simple know Aristotle because your father instructed you to read him?"

"My family is originally from Greece, yes. I was born here in Alexandria though. What about you? How long has your family lived in Alexandria?"

"A long time. Since before the Romans destroyed the temple in Jerusalem, I think. There were already large Jewish communities in the Persian empire before Alexander the Great conquered them. From what I heard my family chose not to return to Judea after the conquest. In hindsight, that was probably a good thing."

"Sadly, I do not know much of the history or religion of your people—except of course that Passover is a rather large event," confessed Hypatia.

"It takes a lot of work for a home to get ready for it! Nearly all of the preparations are done by mothers and their daughters. Men may get the glory, but without us they would be helpless!" smirked Rachel.

"' And Miriam the prophetess, the sister of Aaron, took a tambourine in her hand; and all the women went out after her with tambourines and with dances.'" quoted Hypatia. "Isn't that part of your Torah?"

"Yes … it's from Exodus. How do you know that story?"

Hypatia laughed, "My father is a librarian in the main library. There are Torah scrolls there, you know."

"And so, there are!"

"And so, there are what?" asked a middle aged Jewish man.

Rachel turned and hugged him, "Father! Hypatia and I were just talking about Passover."

The man turned towards Hypatia, "Hypatia, daughter of Theon?"

"Yes."

"I am Levi ben David."

"A pleasure to meet you, Levi. Your daughter does you great credit. You should be very proud."

"I am," affirmed Levi before turning to Rachel, "So, are you ready to head home? Your mother needs your help, I imagine."

Rachel nodded obediently, "Of course, Father. A pleasure meeting you, Hypatia!"

Hypatia saluted them as they turned and walked away. "Salve, Rachel! May we meet again someday."

Spring yielded to summer and summer to autumn. The starry sky wheeled around Alexandria and Hypatia grew into womanhood. Listening to her father lecture his students on Hipparchus of Nicaea, Hypatia sat quietly at a table within the Serapeum, her pen scraping against the blank papyrus as she carefully copied Aristarchus' "On the Sizes and Distances of the Sun and Moon." Pulling out a small measuring device she copied Aristarchus' diagrams precisely, delighting in the beauty of his geometry, her mind half listening to her father's class as she worked.

Aristarchus taught a heliocentric explanation for the motions of the planets and stars using elliptical orbits for the Earth and the celestial wanderers. Yet Hipparchus, writing only a few decades later, found the logic behind Aristarchus' calculations lacking. After all, Nature only allowed for perfectly circular orbits; the idea of an elliptical orbit was utterly absurd! Everyone thought so too. And so, Hipparchus resolved the conflicts created by Earth centrism with a simple tool thought of by Apollonius of Perga: the epicycle. With epicycles the sun, moon, stars, and wanderers travelled in a small circle as they each travelled in a larger circle around the Earth. And besides, under Aristarchus' heliocentric model, the universe became a vast, almost infinitely large space, something Hipparchus absolutely could not accept. For what could man mean to the gods if the universe was vast and expansive? Would not humanity become too insignificant for the gods to care about?

Though her father's lecture spoke only of Hipparchus and his innovative use of triangles in astronomy, Hypatia found herself wondering: what if the problem with Aristarchus was not in his observations, but in the fear by Hipparchus and other devotees of Aristotle's earth centric philosophy that perhaps the gods cared less about humans than the priests taught—if they existed at all? And if the gods did not exist, what then? Was the human reasoning so cherished by the gods sufficient to prosper and thrive without religious belief? Could humans control their own destinies instead of fearing the world around them and yielding authority over their lives to gods and the priests who claimed to speak for them? Was it even safe to contemplate any realm of life where the gods did not rule over every thought, feeling, or decision to be made? Or were her contemplations of an Earth moving around the sun and a world ruled by logic and reason simply begging the gods to strike her down?

As the sun set beneath the horizon, Hypatia could only wonder.

Chapter Three

The city of Athens glittered like a jewel on the Aegean Sea. Now sixteen Hypatia climbed the many Athenian hills until she reached the top Acropolis Hill with its many mighty temples. Soberly she stepped into the Parthenon and gazed at its massive statue of Athena. Skirting the beautiful pool reflecting Athena in her gold and ivory glory, Hypatia sat down next to the sacred water. In the quiet of the temple her mind raced through the many books she'd read, the many contradictory opinions of the great teachers she grew up honouring and respecting. Proofs and equations unfolded through her subconscious like fast moving streams. Songs and stories in all the languages of Alexandria's agora entwined with the mathematics flowing through her. Did Athena speak to her in the language of science? Only one thing was certain: this learning, this knowledge must be protected and preserved for all generations. It was not enough to learn. For the light of knowledge to survive, she must also teach, no matter the cost.

Sunset glowed orange bright. After a day of reflection and a bit of shopping and tourism Hypatia arrived at last at the home of her father's friend and colleague Alexandros. A slave greeted her and ushered her into the well-tended courtyard garden. Alexandros greeted her warming, "Salve! Kaló apógevma! How was your journey?"

"Peaceful. I am staying at the large inn near Acropolis Hill. I hope you do not mind I did not come directly to your beautiful home. The Parthenon beckoned like a siren," smiled Hypatia.

"The goddess has that effect on people, particularly those whose hearts and minds seek wisdom and learning. How is your father?" asked Alexandros.

"Eager to see you again."

"As I am him. Have no fear. I shall make it back to Alexandria, though perhaps not for a year or two." Alexandros studied Hypatia, "You have grown. The last time I visited Theon you were a little girl trying and failing to master the aulos. Please tell me you have improved!"

"Oh, that I could make you such a positive report. But the muses speak not to me in such a fashion. Rather it is the music of the heavens that I hear, the geometry of the sky that speaks to and through me."

"Your father says you have a true gift. Not only for astronomy and geometry, but for understanding the nuances of the written word as well, not to mention for philosophy."

"I am no Homer, no Socrates," blushed Hypatia humbly.

"Homer did not understand trigonometry as you do nor did Socrates appreciate the beauty of many cultures. I heard stories that from time to time you quietly attend worship services at a synagogue. Is it true? Are you converted to the religion of the Jews?"

"I have a friend, Rachel bat Levi. Her father Levi ben David is a cantor. I come to see her and to listen to the beautiful music. Her father has a true gift for singing, as do all in her family. Maybe I cannot play the aulos, but I can appreciate beauty where I find it. Alexandria offers many opportunities to find beauty if one will only open one's heart and mind to see past what is practical or familiar," explained Hypatia.

"So, for you learning is a means unto itself?"

"Absolutely. Knowledge enriches us. What one studies matters less than the pursuit of knowledge. The gods gave us the power to think, to feel, to reason as perhaps their greatest of gifts. It would be disgraceful to not use these gifts to the fullest of one's abilities."

"If only all saw it as you do."

"You are referring to the writings of the Christian Saint Paul? In his letter to the Colossians he wrote, 'See to it that no one takes you captive through hollow and deceptive philosophy, which depends on human tradition and the elemental spiritual forces of this world rather than on Christ. For in Christ all the fullness of the Deity lives in bodily form, and in Christ you have been brought to fullness. He is the head over every power and authority.'"

"You are well-informed! I admit I am surprised by the depth of your study. I know very few people who read and study quite so broadly."

"You honour me."

"Perhaps. Or perhaps I simply recognize greatness when I see it. Come! I would have you share your knowledge with others who pursue learning as you do. We meet every tenth day, gathering together at the Arch of Hadrian. We talk, we debate, sometimes we even compete with one another in physical contests. There are no forbidden topics, no rules we must follow beyond basic decency and civility. I think you would enjoy being part of our community," invited Alexandros.

"Efcharistó, I would be delighted to attend."

"I shall come to your lodging three days hence—unless you would consider staying with me and my family."

"What a kind and generous offer. Tonight, I will sleep at the inn, but in the morning, I shall return and stay with you for the remainder of my time in Athens—

or until you bid me depart should you find me insufferable," teased Hypatia.

"Until tomorrow then!"

Hypatia thrived in Alexandros' group of young Neoplatonists. As he promised, no subject was forbidden, no writer banished from discussion. As Hypatia learned and grew she found her reputation rising, not only among her Neoplatonist friends, but across scholarly circles across Athens and beyond. Night fell on her seventeenth year and her eighteenth birthday approached Hypatia boarded a ship for home optimistic that her time in Greece was well-spent.

"Fire! Fire!" cried the night watchman as flames shot up through the roof of the Great Library. Though many small fires had destroyed parts of the Library over the centuries, this fire burnt with historic fierceness, lighting up the Great Harbour and blocking the stars as if it were noon and not approaching midnight. Hypatia watched dozens of men, including her father, plunged themselves into the burning building in attempt to save what precious few manuscripts they could. Not all who entered the inferno came back again. Hypatia handed cups of water to the firefighters, doing what she could to support them.

By morning, not a single stone remaining upon another. This time there could be no rebuilding, no rededication to Zeus, Athena, or Serapis. The light of knowledge was going out. Now only the branch libraries in the Caesareum and in the Temple of Serapis remained of what was once the greatest collection of manuscripts and books the western world had ever known. Hypatia walked among the ruins; a great wave of emotion filled her. Shaking, she fell to the ground, a soulful scream bursting from the depths of her being as an ocean of tears poured out from her eyes. Was this what the Jews felt when the Romans pulled down their temple in Jerusalem? Was this the reason why Rachel wept at Passover each time someone proclaimed, "Next year in Jerusalem?"

"I thought you might be here," soothed a familiar voice behind her.

Hypatia looked up and took the hand offered to her, "You came!"

Rachel pulled Hypatia to her feet, "Where else would my favourite gentile be but among the ashes of the books she loves so deeply?"

"You know me well!"

"Shall I ask my rabbi to say a prayer for you?"

"Not for me, but for all learning, all wisdom. The light must not go out, Rachel! I don't want to live in a world where learning is forbidden and scholars are mocked as madmen."

"It will not go out, Hypatia, not as long as you have the courage to defend the light, to teach what you know, and discover what you may using the gifts Yahweh has bestowed upon you."

"You believe science is a gift from your God as well as mine?"

"What does it matter how we worship or where, what names we use? As long as we are good and kind and help one another, that is what matters," affirmed Rachel. "And yes, I do believe science comes from God. Why give us the ability to learn and study if such things were unholy?" Pausing, Rachel wiped the tears from Hypatia's face, "Come now! I will walk with you back home."

Chapter Four

"All hail Theophilus, Patriarch of Alexandria!" cried Cyril proudly as the ceremony elevating his uncle to patriarch concluded.

Proudly Theophilus processed out of the cathedral and into the street beyond where a large adoring crowd gathered to honour him. Theophilus raised his hands victoriously, "Good Christians I welcome you! Those who are faithful to the true religion, the true teachings of our Lord Jesus Christ! Today we celebrate! For now, we shall purge from our number those who claim to follow Jesus but will not follow His words! We will not tolerate those who say our Lord spoke in metaphor nor those who question whether or not all of the words scripture apply to all people and for eternity! No! Either you believe in the word of God or you do not! Either you fight and live and die for Jesus or you are a pagan heathen, a barbarian, an animal to be sacrificed. Are you ready to cleanse the Church? I cannot hear you! Are you ready? Are you ready to receive salvation from your sins? Follow me! Follow me and I will show you the kingdom of God! I will take you to paradise!"

The crowd shouted. The crowd stamped their feet. The crowd beat swords upon shields, the noise rippling through the city like an earthquake ready to shake walls from their foundations. This pageantry was no simple spectacle to celebrate another patriarch's elevation. This time no centurions would come to defend those targeted by the mob. This time the legions sided with the mob. Those who dared disagree with the mob would be slain.

"Alexandros! You have returned at last!" greeted Hypatia.

Alexandros embraced her, "I have news!"

Hypatia beckoned him to sit down, "Oh?"

"There was a gathering of Neoplatonists here in Alexandria; you are quiet the rising star! Your commentaries on both Apollonius' 'Conics' and on Diophantus' 'Arithmetica' are being widely copied across the Empire. At a mere thirty-five years old, you are now one of the most cherished and respected philosophers and teachers in all of the Roman Empire! History will remember you in the same way they remember Homer and Socrates and Plato!"

"Spoken like a mentor proud of his student!" quipped Hypatia.

"You think I exaggerate?"

"I think I have built upon my father's work and legacy more than created one for myself. If credit must be given, give it to the great Theon of Alexandria, not his progeny."

"Your students disagree," countered Alexandros.

"Logically," asserted Hypatia. "For if they did not consider my words worth hearing they would not pay to hear them nor waste their time to do so."

"True," conceded Alexandros. "Now let us drink and be merry for it has been far too many years since last we dined together."

"Welcome to Alexandria and the Temple of Serapis," greeted Hypatia. "I am Hypatia, daughter of Theon."

Synesius of Cyrene bowed to her, "It is an honour to meet you at last. You do not know how much I have desired to come to Alexandria to study with you."

"Your words do me credit," bowed Hypatia politely as she led the way towards her classroom. "I can only hope you find the lessons as valuable as you hoped."

Ten minutes later Synesius and Hypatia strode into her modest classroom. As Hypatia took her place in front, Synesius sat down in the second row next to a well-dressed Roman in a toga. The Roman turned to him, "You are new."

"I am," confirmed Synesius. "Synesius of Cyrene."

"Orestes, aide to our Roman legatus—for the time being at any rate."

"Meaning?"

"Meaning our Orientis Praefecto has a habit of changing who represents him in Alexandria. It can be no wonder this city is always two steps away from erupting in chaos," explained Orestes. "It's worse than ever now that Theophilus is patriarch of the Christian archdiocese. The church could not have picked a greater agent of chaos and violence if they had dragged down to Earth one of those wild German gods and set him free to council with Prometheus himself!"

"Orestes, are you ready for class to begin?" asked Hypatia.

Slightly chided, Orestes nodded, "Yes, my lady. Sorry my lady."

"No harm done," winked Hypatia. "Now let us resume our discussion about Aristarchus and Hipparchus. Both were brilliant natural philosophers and mathematicians. Both contributed to our understanding of the universe and the mind of Creator. But both explained what they observed very differently using two completely different models.

"Plato called the universe the 'Spindle of Necessity.' He did not believe in natural laws and saw the changes in brightness in the sun, moon, and wanderers and the erratic motion of the wanderers themselves as proof that the gods are in charge, not natural laws. Hipparchus agreed with Plato that the Earth is the centre of the universe.

"But Aristarchus saw the universe very differently. Observing the size of the Earth's shadow during a lunar eclipse convinced Aristarchus that the sun must be much larger than the moon and that the sun and stars are fixed with the Earth, moon, and wanderers moving around the sun which is, itself, simply one of countless stars. Putting the sun at the centre easily accounts for the erratic motion of the wanderers."

"But what about the differences in the size and brightness of the sun, moon, and wanderers?" asked Synesius. "If these orbits are all circular then you cannot possibly explain these variations."

"True," agreed Hypatia, "but this problem exists whether you put the Earth or the sun at the centre. With Aristarchus' model you resolve this problem by moving the centre of each orbit so that the Earth, moon, and wanderers are travelling in ellipses. This was something even Aristarchus himself was not ready to do and indeed there is evidence to believe he abandoned his own heliocentric model and returned to Plato's Earth-centrism.

"Enter in Hipparchus. Writing a little more than one hundred years later, Hipparchus tested Aristarchus' heliocentric model and rejected it for two reasons. Firstly, he could not reconcile the idea of elliptical orbits, but secondly and perhaps most interestingly from a philosophical point of view, Hipparchus noticed that under Aristarchus' model the universe becomes infinite in size. And if the universe is massive, how can the gods exist or if they do, why would they care about the actions of humanity? A massively large universe leaves no place for the gods or for humanity's place in the universe? Humanity becomes irrelevant, tiny, unimportant. And so, in rejecting Aristarchus, Hipparchus returned to the Earth centric model and here he found the perfect solution to the problem of the retrograde motion of the wanderers and the changes in brightness. Who knows what he added?"

"Epicycles," answered Orestes.

"Explain to us all, what is an epicycle, Orestes?" questioned Hypatia.

"It's an orbit within an orbit."

Hypatia smiled, "Correct! With epicycles all the motions of the sun, moon, stars, and wanderers fit perfectly and the gods remain the gods. The conflicts are all resolved –or are they?" asked Hypatia. "For in deciding whether the Earth, moon, and wanderers move around the sun in elliptical orbits or if the Earth is the fixed centre of the universe with everything else moving around it we are making decisions about the nature of God and God's mind. Does God think in terms of simplicity or in terms of perfect geometry? If the universe is created to function simply and efficiently, we must challenge long cherished beliefs and adopt heliocentrism with its massive universe and the possibility that there are worlds and civilizations on those worlds above and beyond what we know on Earth. But if perfect geometry matters to God, we must accept the epicycles and a more complex set of rules to govern the motions of the heavens. I cannot tell you what to believe. But I can tell you that whatever answer speaks to your heart will place you closer to the mind and heart of God and the bliss that awaits when our minds touch the sacred. Let us meditate and pray on this. Class dismissed."

Chapter Five

December arrived crisp and merry to Alexandria. Slaves decorated their masters' homes with bright green garlands. Masters and mistresses gave each slave money to spend on Saturnalia gifts. Vast quantities of wine emerged from cellars or were delivered to homes by wine merchants. Cooks and chefs candied fruits, baked sweets, and prepared a staggering number of dishes for the Saturnalia feasts. In the home of Theon, Hypatia wrapped special candles custom made for each of her students. Upon each parcel, she attached a tiny scroll onto which she wrote out an inspiring quote or sentiment. On the gift for Orestes she wrote simply, "Defend the Light." On the gift for Synesius she wrote, "Do not forget me."

That afternoon Hypatia took a long stroll through the city. Arriving at the door to the home of Asher ben Nathan she smiled as a servant responded to the door bell, 'Chag Urim Sameach!"

"Salve!" smiled the servant opening the door. "I am Daphne. I serve my mistress Rachel bat Levi. You must be Hypatia."

"I am," confirmed Hypatia. Following Daphne into the living room she studied the servant's appearance, "I see no mark of ownership; are you a paid servant?"

"Yes. My master bought me as a wedding gift to my mistress, but she freed me and offered to pay me wages if I would stay with her and help her, particularly during Shabbat and the holidays. The offer was quite generous and I am happy to be part of this family," explained Daphne as she motioned for Hypatia to sit down.

Five minutes later Rachel entered the living room, her son and two daughters following close behind and being watched over by Daphne. Hypatia rose and embraced her friend, "Chag Urim Sameach!"

"Chag Urim Sameach!" smiled Rachel. "You remember my children: Ruth, Batia, and Nathan."

"I haven't seen Nathan since his brit milah three years ago. My goodness he has grown!" laughed Hypatia.

"Ruth will be ten years old next week, if you can believe it!"

"She was born during Saturnalia, wasn't she?"

"Yes, and Batia was born on Yom Kippur just over eight years ago."

"Ruth is your mother-in-law's name?"

"You have a great memory! How goes your classes? I heard you took on an aide to the Roman legate. What's his name?"

"Orestes. Ambitious young man. I think he wants to become prefect. Doesn't matter if it's here in the east or one of the other prefectures."

"Why stop at prefect? Why not take the throne from Theodosius and declare himself emperor?"

"Don't tempt him," smirked Hypatia. Looking down for a moment she remembered the gift she carried with her, "Oh before I forget … this is for you!"

Taking the wrapped gift from Hypatia, Rachel unwrapped it carefully to reveal a finely wrought silver menorah, "It's beautiful!"

"It's made to precisely comply with design specified in Exodus twenty-five, right down to the almond leaves, cups, and branches. There is a story I heard that the almond tree is sacred to the feminine part of the divine. In Judea, they've even found an ancient stone that says, 'May Yahweh and his Asherah bless you.'

"Some say Asherah was God's consort. Others say she was His equal, creatrix of the universe and the reason why there is often a plural in Genesis in the creation story. If your ancestors did once worship a creatrix then they have much more in common with the peoples of Gaul, Britannia, and Germania than they do their Greek and Roman conquerors."

"An intriguing idea, isn't it," added Rachel. "My father is coming tonight for dinner and to light the second candle. You are welcome to join us."

"Asher won't mind?"

"Mind me inviting my old friend to dinner? No. Besides, as a rabbi he might have some things to discuss with you."

"What sorts of things?"

"Theophilus for one."

"Should I invite Orestes to come then? Or do you prefer we keep the Romans out of this one?"

"If you invite Orestes then you must invite Synesius as well. From your letters he seems quite amiable," noted Rachel.

"Amiable and perhaps a little bit in love with his teacher."

"Was he the one you gave your rag to?"

"No, no that was years ago. A different student. He caught my meaning well enough. Young men think that love and romance is all pretty songs, poetry, and dancing without thinking about the realities of life with women. I set that one in his place on the matter and reminded him of the contradictions between his words to me and his beliefs about the nature of women. If God is kind to Synesius he will set his heart on another woman, one his own age, and love me as a mother and a mentor."

A few hours later sunset burned rose-orange over the house of Asher ben Nathan. As promised, Hypatia returned with both Orestes and Synesius one pace behind her. Reaching the dining room Orestes offered a bottle of wine to Rachel, "Thank you for inviting us. I hope you do not mind. I found this at a wine merchant a few blocks away. He assured me that it was suitable for your table and approved by the rabbinate."

Rachel looked at the label before handing it off to her husband, "A fine vintage most generously given. Asher and I drank this vintage at our wedding. It has very special memories!"

"My lady said this was the right one to buy," remarked Orestes.

"Hypatia has an excellent memory."

"Yes, she does," agreed Asher. "Daphne, will you prepare the wine for our dinner?"

Daphne took the bottle, "Of course, my lord!"

Asher beckoned everyone to sit while he stood, "Baruch Atah Adonai Elohenu Melech Ha-olam, asher kidshanu b'mitzvotav v'tzivanu l'hadlik ner shel Hanukkah. Blessed is Adonai, our God, Ruler of the Universe, who hallows us with mitzvot and commands us to kindle the Hanukkah lights. Baruch Atah Adonai Elohenu Melech Ha-olam,she-asa nissim la-avotenu ba-yamim ha-mem ba-z'man ha-zeh. Blessed is Adonai, our God, Ruler of the Universe, who performed wondrous deed for our ancestors in days of old, at this season." Prayerfully he lit the first and second candle, "Tonight as we celebrate Hanukkah together, we are conscious of the precious gift of family and friendship. So often we take one another for granted, forgetting to express our love and devotion. As we kindle these festive lights, let us rededicate ourselves to sharing our interests and time with one another. Like the Maccabees of old, let us always face the troubles and joys of life united by those we love."

"Amen," answered Rachel and her children.

"Amen," echoed the guests.

Rachel turned to her husband, "Asher, Hypatia was kind enough to give us a beautiful menorah. Shall we light it as well?"

Asher kissed her, "Certainly, matok!" Rising he fetched Hypatia's menorah from the living room and put it on the dining room table in front of everyone. Daphne brought in a set of candles which Asher set into each cup expertly. Lighting the shamash candle for Hypatia's menorah from the shamash on the original menorah, he lit the first two candles, "Baruch Atah Adonai Elohenu Melech Ha-olam, asher kidshanu b'mitzvotav v'tzivanu l'hadlik ner shel Hanukkah."

Orestes studied the gifted menorah, "You gave this to them, my lady?"

"Yes, why?"

"I recognize the craftsmanship. It was made by the finest silversmith in Alexandria."

Hypatia as she took a sip from her wine glass, "Nothing is too good for my dear friend Rachel. We've been friends since childhood."

"My lady is truly most generous," added Synesius.

"Jew, Christian, Pagan—there is no difference between us," asserted Hypatia. "We are all in search of truth beyond human understanding, with a greater connection to the Divine. Does it truly matter what name or names we use, what languages we speak, or how we worship? Surely God or the gods care less about how we worship than how we live. Actions, not words, matter most."

"Theophilus disagrees," declared Synesius. "For him and his followers everyone must believe and worship in accord with his ideas of orthodoxy. There is only one true belief, only one way of correctly worshipping. He preaches in the agora a most fiery and impassioned manifesto, one that often calls for enforcement of Christian orthodoxy upon those who disagree with it—Christian, Jew, or Pagan—all must live, worship, and believe as he interprets the Bible."

"Has anyone of his congregants acted on his words?" asked Rachel.

"Not yet, but they may sooner rather than later. Saturnalia is nearly upon us," answered Synesius.

Rachel stared at Synesius, "Saturnalia? I do not understand the significance in this context."

Asher's face grew grim, "In the Empire, Saturnalia is often a time for murder. Many promotions come out of Saturnalia assassinations."

"Will the legate intervene?" asked Rachel.

Orestes met Rachel's eyes, "It depends on who is killed or at least targeted and who the attacker is. The legate is a politician first. If there is nothing to gain and something to lose by acting you can be certain he will do nothing."

"Orestes is right about the legate. I can easily see him standing by and allowing one or more than one of Theophilus' congregants get away with murder," affirmed Hypatia.

"Will he attack the school at the Temple of Serapis?" asked Rachel.

"Possible, but not likely," answered Asher. "It's too big a target and he lacks sufficient support to get away with it—for now, at least. Burn the temple or the Caesareum and he'll have to answer to the prefect for it. No, he won't move against either, not yet. Saturnalia violence is small-scale. An attack on any institution like your school costs him too much right now to try. But I promise you this: the moment the prefect and his legates waiver in their protection, our houses of worship and houses of learning will fall to Theophilus and his frenzied thugs he calls Christians."

Saturnalia arrived bright and green to the house of Theon. Sitting together as equals with his slaves around the dining room table, Theon sat and watched as they exchanged the gifts they bought for one another before opening a large basket full of gifts. To some slaves he gave money, to others he gave beautiful ornaments for their clothing and bodies, and to still others he gave materials to use for making personal items of their own design and choosing. To Hypatia he gave her a finely wrought bronze astrolabe. Hypatia hugged her father warmly, "Efcharistó!"

"You've been teaching so much of late you have barely had any time for your research," observed Theon.

"I know," conceded Hypatia. "The price of popularity, I suppose. All the more necessary each day Theophilus gains more power and the government wanes in its protections of our long-cherished institutions. Next the government will rescind its policies towards educating girls and restrict access to schools to boys and men. The one truly good thing to come out of the Roman Empire will be gone."

"Surely you do not believe educating girls is the only good thing the Romans ever did."

"Perhaps, perhaps not. Perhaps I am not the person to ask. Perhaps the best judges of that are in Gaul, in Britannia, Germania, and all the other provinces who lost their culture, their language, even their religions to the legions. Would the killer queen Boudicca be happy with Roman Britannia? Surely not."

"Roman Britannia is fading away. It is too far, too expensive to keep the legions there. Every year more and more soldiers are recalled from Britannia back to the continent. Soon the western empire will be gone and only the eastern emperor will remain. Our world is changing and not for the better, Hypatia. Soon perhaps all learning will be gone and with it the light that has preserved and protected our people and all peoples from the violence of the mob," forecasted Theon.

"Which is why I must teach. We must defend the light against this darkness. The more students I teach—" Hypatia stopped suddenly. A loud banging sounded on the front door. Dutifully a slave went to answer it. Hypatia heard muffled voices, then heard the slave escort the visitor into the living room. Horrified Hypatia saw Rachel covered in blood and soot, "What happened?!"

Rachel staggered. A slave brought her a chair and a cup of wine. Rachel wept, "Asher and the children are dead. I barely escaped."

"What?"

"Our home is gone. Theophilus' thugs. They came; muttered something from their Bible about Jews and Jews as the killers of their Christ. Then they—they…"

Hypatia sat down beside Rachel, the smell of her burned flesh making Hypatia's stomach queasy, "What happened? You can tell me."

"I am despoiled," confessed Rachel hysterically. "They did it in front of my children before they slit their throats. They tortured Asher before—then they stole all our precious things and when they had looted everything of value to them they set fire to our house and the houses of all the Jews."

Hypatia stood up and walked outside her door. Looking eastward towards the Jewish quarter she saw the entire district in a blaze of red, yellow, orange and black. Smoke and the smell of burning flesh assaulted her until she was driven inside, "My God!"

Theon knelt beside Rachel with a bowl of cold water and a sponge and began to dab the water onto her burns, "I will send for my physician at once. He does not need to know who you really are."

"Won't he guess I am a Jew from these injuries?"

"If he does I will pay him to keep that quiet. As of right now you are our cousin. You will live here under our roof and protection for as long as it is ours to offer."

The twenty-fifth of December came. As the western empire celebrated the birth of Jesus Christ, Theophilus celebrated his victory against the Jews in Alexandria, a victory made sweeter by the lack of response by the prefect. As Orestes and Hypatia predicted neither the prefect nor his legates in Alexandria moved against Theophilus. Empowered, Theophilus decided to give the Eastern Church a mighty gift for the nativity of Jesus Christ in January. He would cleanse the city of Serapis and all its old gods and goddesses to make the city a Christian city. No matter the cost.

Chapter Six

"My lady! My lady!" cried Synesius as he pounded on the front door to Theon's home. The slave opened the door; Synesius rushed to Hypatia, "My lady! We must hurry but not seem as if we are hurrying."

Hypatia draped her palla over her shoulders, "What is happening, Synesius?"

"Theophilus is planning on destroying the Caesareum and the Temple of Serapis."

"What? When?"

"Two days from now, as soon as Christmas celebrations are finished. He said we will purge Alexandria of all its pagan filth and pagan books just as we have started to purge its Jewish filth from the land," reported Synesius with fear and urgency in his voice.

Worried Hypatia stood and pondered for a moment, "Can you gather the other students together? Quietly organize them to withdraw as many books as possible—without it looking like we are doing anything other than a major research project. Tell the attending librarians I am beginning a new research project and need as many copies of as many books as possible for my work. Have the books sent here—as many as you can save from both libraries if you can, but if you cannot then focus on the library at the Temple of Serapis. No one will suspect anything if you and the others are seen there. I will see Orestes and see what he can do to help us."

Fifteen minutes later Hypatia entered the legate's office. Orestes greeted her, "Hypatia, what a lovely surprise. What can I do for you this morning?"

"Synesius has not come to see you?"

"No, why?"

"Theophilus has ordered the destruction of the Caesareum and the Temple of Serapis. We need your help, Orestes. Will the legate act against Theophilus officially?"

"We can arrange a meeting between the legate, Theophilus, and yourself if you like. That much I can do for you," offered Orestes.

"Schedule it for the day after tomorrow and not a minute before, Orestes. He must not know that we know his plans. I have no wish to endanger Synesius' life which surely must be forfeit if anyone close to the patriarch knew he was our source of information."

"Synesius is a colleague and able orator. I would never wish him harmed. Of course, I will keep this quiet for you. If I know you there's already a counter measure in the works that you would be wise to keep from me until it is safe."

"Am I that predictable?" asked Hypatia.

"Only to those who love you best, my lady!" grinned Orestes.

Hypatia furtively walked to the library in the Temple of Serapis. Covering her head with her palla she avoided the common places where students gathered and took a direct route. Finally, she reached the central dome. A dozen of her students busied themselves with selecting books and placing them in large baskets. Once full, a layer of linen was placed over the precious manuscripts over which a layer of bread was added to add to the illusion. Each basket was then loaded to a wagon which could transport from four to six baskets at a time and delivered to the house of Theon.

After two hours Rachel slipped into the library; Hypatia loaded her arms with books and carefully carried them to another basket, "I have news about the library at the Caesareum."

"How goes the work there?" asked Hypatia.

"I am sorry to say we were only able to save a few dozen books. Christian soldiers have figured out what we are doing. We have very little time left, perhaps only what you can bring out on this wagon and even then, we might be betrayed," reported Rachel.

"Go to Orestes and work with him to create a diversion. If this is the last trip we can make let us at very least make it a successful one," ordered Hypatia.

Twenty minutes later Hypatia heard a raucous noise coming from the street. Women and men shouted angrily. Hypatia turned to her students, "Whatever we have right now is all we can save. Let's load these up and leave while Rachel's diversion persists."

"I'll guide the wagon," volunteered Synesius.

"No," objected Hypatia. "If some problem should arise you will be discovered and your life forfeit."

"Or my standing in the Christian community might save these books. Please, my lady, let me try. I'm willing to risk my life to defend the light. How many in Alexandria can say the same?" begged Synesius.

"Very well," conceded Hypatia, "but be careful!"

Synesius bowed as he picked up the final basket, "Always!"

"Where are you taking that?" barked Orestes from his horse.

Synesius pretended not to know him, "I am on an errand on behalf of my lady. These baskets must be delivered or her Christmas party will be remembered as the worst Christmas celebration in the history of the city!"

Orestes drew his gladius, "Really? And why should believe you?"

"I am a Christian. I would never lie," declared Synesius loudly.

"Christians used to be sport for the games," countered Orestes.

"Christianity is the way of the empire now. Does the legate contradict his own prefect on this matter?"

"No, but that doesn't mean I trust you either. Very well, you declare these baskets are for your lady. I will escort you to her home with these baskets. Then we shall decide who is telling the truth!" shouted Orestes, mindful his armed escort was listening carefully. Orestes turned to the soldiers with him, "You there! Make sure no one intervenes—from within the Temple or beyond."

"Sir, yes sir!" saluted the soldiers; Synesius returned to the wagon's driver seat and nudged the reins, Orestes riding next to him on his fine horse.

Finally, after several minutes they arrived at the house of Theon. Slaves quickly unloaded the wagon.

One by one Hypatia's students slipped into the back door, most of them carrying hidden treasures from the temple. After another twenty tense minutes Hypatia slipped into her living room and pulled out a menorah triumphantly, "Look what I recovered!"

Orestes stared in wonder, "That menorah looks very familiar!"

"It should. It's the one I gave Rachel for Hanukkah. I found it!"

"Found what?" asked Rachel as she walked through the door. Staring at the menorah she fell to her knees in shock, "What? How?"

"Not all of Theophilus' followers think of me as some evil sorceress bewitching our leaders with my demon-inspired philosophy! I asked and my wish was granted. Or more precisely, I was able to buy it back for a generous donation to his parish. Some of Theophilus' followers actually do care about following the teachings of Jesus when it comes to feeding and providing shelter for the poor. They are not all thugs," acknowledged Hypatia. "Now, if you are all ready, let's get these books secured and hidden away. Orestes if you wish to appear neutral I think it wise for you to be elsewhere while we work."

Orestes nodded, "I will ride back to the legate's office and see what can be done. Expect me when you see me."

Two days later Orestes, Hypatia, and Patriarch Theophilus assembled in the legate's office, Theophilus noticeably annoyed, "Can we get this over with please? It's Christmas and I have duties that simply cannot wait!"

"Duties involving the Caesareum?" asked the legate.

"Of course not!" denied Theophilus.

"Do you also deny you are responsible for the burning of Jewish homes and businesses during Saturnalia?" asked Hypatia.

"Now why would I do that? The Jews are our neighbours and friends," argued Theophilus, "though not perhaps as good a friend to Christians as they are to you, my lady."

Orestes stepped forward in Hypatia's defence, "The Lady Hypatia is not on trial, Your Holiness."

"The Lady Hypatia is far too friendly with the most ungodly of people. Perchance she is not as virtuous as you Romans believe," suggested Theophilus.

"Or perhaps she is a better Christian than you are," offered Orestes.

"Gentlemen, please!" rebuffed the legate. "Enough of this. Theophilus, I have asked you here because there is word that you are continuing to preach violence and mayhem that threatens the lives and property of this city. Do you deny it?"

"I deny the truth of anything that comes out of the mouth of that whore," attacked Theophilus. "As for the rest, I will do what I have always done: follow my conscience. No man can be asked to do more. Now, if you will excuse me, I have business to attend to. Kalá Christoúgenna, felicem natalem Christi to you all."

Orestes stopped him, "We are not done, Theophilus."

Theophilus glared at him, "Yes, we are—unless I am arrested. I would think carefully about arresting the Patriarch of Alexandria without irrefutable proof. Do you have proof that I am guilty of a crime? I can see from your faces that you do not. Very good then, I wish you good day!" Triumphantly, Theophilus marched out of the legate's office.

Orestes watched him angrily. The legate put his hand on Orestes' shoulder, "We tried. I know how much this means to you, Orestes. But he's right: there's nothing we can do, not without proof he's conspiring against this city."

"Letting Theophilus get away with this is a mistake, my lord. He is guilty of inciting mobs to abuse the Jewish community. Whatever violence is coming to this city, he will be the mastermind planning on that. Of that you can be absolutely certain," affirmed Hypatia.

Three hours later church bells sounded the alarm. Fire! Fire! Fire! Cries swelled up across the city. Flames pierced the domes of both the Caesareum and the Temple of Serapis as Christian Roman soldiers defended the mobs sweeping through both complexes. Flaming arrows shot through the air to ignite library stacks and rooftops. Armed men with clubs and swords hacked at the stones and slaughtered any who dared oppose them. Theon and Hypatia watched with sadness and horror as the world they knew and loved fell to ashes. The classical world of the philosopher, the scholar, the scientist was gone, replaced by the zealot eager to please his bishop at the expense of all else that lived, breathed, or dared think. The roaring bonfire of knowledge that was Alexandria was now reduced to a flickering and fragile candle, a small but precious candle being tended only by those who dared risk their lives to defend the light.

Chapter Seven

Patriarch Theophilus wasted no time in implementing his plans for Alexandria. With both the Caesareum and the Temple of Serapis a pile of rubble and ash workers arrived to both sites to build churches in their place, the Roman legate complacently permitting Theophilus and his followers to act without interference from the government. Zealots swept through the entire city in search of statues, precious objects, and secret worship sites belonging to Greek, Roman, and Egyptian religions. In Rome, Emperor Theodosius dissolved the vestal virgins and banned all traditional, "pagan" rituals at the Olympic games. One by one, piece by piece, each move banned the classical world into memory.

"Must you go?" asked Hypatia tearfully as Synesius packed the last of his belongings onto the passenger ship in the harbour where his wife and children waited for him.

Synesius held her close, "My time in Alexandria is at an end. I am married now and must take care of my family. Cyrene will be a better place for my boys. I fear Alexandria is too dangerous now. Surely, my lady, you can understand that I must think of their well-being. I cannot be so selfish as to stay in your company forever!"

"Will you write me?"

"Try to stop me, my lady! For as long as I have breath I will remember you and write to you. Our story is not over; it has simply moved to a different chapter," consoled Synesius. With a finger he wiped a tear from her cheek. Hypatia held him close. Synesius kissed her sweetly, "I love you."

"I love you too, Synesius. May God keep you safe!"

Synesius kissed her one final time, "And you, my lady!"

Five years later, Hypatia watched the flames cover her father's body. Theon of Alexandria was dead. Of all the classical philosophers of Alexandria only she remained to defend the light of knowledge to the next generation of students who quietly came to her home to study outside of the prying eyes of the patriarch.

As promised Synesius wrote to her, keeping her abreast of the many changes in his life, including his election to Bishop of Ptolemais. To Hypatia's great pleasure Synesius built upon his lessons from Hypatia, engaging in scientific research in his own right and experimenting with new and better scientific instruments. Hypatia's light and reputation around the world was spreading even as the light flickered in Alexandria itself.

"Thank you, that will be all," commanded Orestes to his guards as he arrived at the house of Hypatia. Obediently, his guards saluted and turned away. A slave opened the front door and led him into the court yard where Hypatia's many guests, many of them current or former students, assembled and dined on light appetizers prepared for them.

Hypatia greeted Orestes warmly, "My lord prefect! You arrive at last!"

Orestes hugged and kissed her affectionately, "'Praefectus augustalis' is for other people. To you I am simply Orestes."

"As you wish, Orestes," smiled Hypatia.

Orestes looked around him, "This is quite the party already. I recognize some the most prominent members of Alexandrian society here."

"My father is gone, but nothing is changed."

"Well something has changed. Synesius isn't here."

"I think Synesius has his hands full as bishop in Cyrene," observed Hypatia.

"Did they let him stay with his family?"

"At length, yes, though I doubt we will see many married bishops, not if patriarchs like Theophilus get their way. Speaking of which, I heard you were baptized."

"Conditional to my promotion, my lady. I haven't turned away from your lessons. I'm still a Neo-Platonist seeking truth through the esoteric doctrines of the mysteries. The 'eye buried within us' still guides me to the divine, just as you taught. I simply do not remind the rabbis and the Christian clergy of that fact. You taught me the diplomatic arts, after all! I have never seen you turn any student away. Not in any classroom and not in your informal lessons in the agora for that matter! Male, female, old, young, Egyptian, Greek, Jew, Roman, barbarian; you teach any and all who come to you. Language, religion, culture; none of it matters to you. You taught us that learning is for everyone, not just for a few elites."

"If only everyone shared my views on this. I worry for the future, Orestes. Your predecessor was ambivalent at best towards the increasing violence instigated by orthodox Christians, most of them followers of patriarchs like Theophilus. They bully, harass, even kill anyone accused of believing differently than they do, innocent or guilty does not matter to them. They have no sense of honour or mercy. The babe in arms, the lame, the widow, they are all equally targeted as if they were vigorous men able to defend themselves. Even if they are Christian, they are still slaughtered by these so-called soldiers of Christ. You must stand up for them, Orestes! The state must be in charge over the mob."

"I agree with you in principle, my lady," confirmed Orestes.

"But …"

"…but Theophilus has a massive following. People are more loyal to him than they are the empire. Given the mess of things in both Rome and Constantinople, I don't blame those who put more faith in the word of the patriarch of Alexandria than they do the Praefectus augustalis of Egypt."

"Orestes, you are the prefect. You are the government. For the sake of everyone, you must take a stand and govern! Show them why the empire was the most feared power on Earth if you have to. You cannot let this land fall into lawlessness. We are not barbarians—are we?" asked Hypatia quietly.

"You don't know what you are asking of me."

"Yes, I do. I'm asking you to defend the light of goodness and peace. There was a time when you were eager to do so. Has your heart changed?"

"Perhaps I have grown more conservative of late," conceded Orestes. "It is easy to run out onto the streets with your gladius drawn when you think yourself immortal. Not so easy when you understand how easily death comes to the bold and the brave."

"If you will not protect the innocent, who will, Orestes? Who will defend the light if not you? Why have the power to help others if you will not wield it?"

Orestes kissed her, "Once more you make sense, my lady. Too much sense for my own good. I will … use the time remaining at the party to negotiate what I may to help the most vulnerable if I can."

"See that you do!"

"All hail his holiness, Cyril, Patriarch of Alexandria!" shouted the herald triumphantly as the newly elevated patriarch marched into the city from the church built over the old Caesareum.

Cyril raised his hands to the adoring crowd around him, "My uncle Theophilus has gone to paradise to the bosom of Jesus Christ. Yet his work remains unfinished! Alexandria is not yet a truly Christian city. Since this church's completion eleven years ago we have hoped and prayed for all to turn to eternal salvation. Yet some persist. They cling to their idols, yeah even the Jews who refuse to bow down to Jesus as the Messiah! Killers of Christ with hardened hearts they are!

"But together we will change that. We will drive the heathen from their devil worship. We will purge all the ancient enchantments and spells from their blackened hearts. We will prove to these pagans that there is but one God, one salvation through our Lord Jesus Christ. And we will drive the devil out of our churches. The devil corrupts us. He lies to us. He tells us that there are many paths to God, many ways to salvation. But there is one and only one. One God. One Salvation. One true belief. If any refuse to believe, they shall be purged so that true Christians will never again be tempted by their devil-worshipping ways nor corrupted by their example! Are you with me? Will you be a soldier of Christ?"

"I will!" shouted one man from the crowd.

"I will!" shouted another, then another, then another until the entire crowd shouted with zealous rage, their stamping feet like an earthquake upon the cobblestone streets.

"Come now," beckoned Patriarch Cyril. The Jews are planning on murdering us. But we will get them first! Follow me!"

From her rooftop Hypatia watched the frenzied mob run from the Caesareum to the Jewish quarter where they killed every Jew they could find. A vision of the future passed before her eyes. "I understand," she answered, "though it cost me my life I will continue to teach. I will continue to stand up for the innocent, even if it means challenging the most powerful men of this age. I will not relent. I will not stand down. If it is my fate to die defending the light, I will. I swear to you, I will!"

Two hours later a letter arrived for Hypatia from Cyrene. Bishop Synesius was dead. Was the vision a message from Synesius? Hypatia could only wonder and pray.

"My lords, my lords, quiet please!" shouted Orestes as leaders from Alexandria's Jewish community shouted insults and accusations towards Cyril and his delegation. From the perimeter of the room Hypatia watched the chaos, ready to step in if Orestes needed her to, but not until then.

"I swear my lord we are innocent of these charges," asserted Cyril. "It is the Jews who want Christians dead! Every day they plot to kill us as they did to kill our Lord Jesus Christ. They are a race of murderers and thieves! How else did they become so prosperous? How else can they afford the finery they display so shamelessly. It is blood money! We Christians are in peril if we do not stop these Jews!"

"Murderers? Murderers? You stone old women walking the streets to come to Shabbat. And when her sons come to demand payment for the doctor, you stone them as well or take up a sword against them," retorted the rabbi. "It is intolerable! My lord prefect you must punish this bishop and his men!"

"You cannot seriously believe the word of Jew!" cried Cyril as Orestes rubbed his temples, his migraine flaring.

Hypatia stepped forward, "Why not? My best friend was a Jew. She's dead now, stoned by your parabalanoi as she left my house on an errand."

"Still listening to this witch, Orestes?" attacked Cyril. "Perhaps she has you under her pagan spell. Perhaps she enchants you with her feminine wiles in her bed chamber! Whore!"

At the final insult Orestes found his courage, "No one insults the virtue of The Philosopher. She is as pure as a vestal virgin!"

"The vestal virgins were disbanded by the emperor," reminded Cyril. "You talk like a pagan when you mention them."

"You talk as if all pagans are evil," countered Orestes. "No, my lord. As long as I am alive, you will desist from insulting the lady Hypatia. You will also desist in preaching against the Jews and inciting violence. Am I clear?"

"I see the lust in your eyes, Orestes! I know how you sin in your heart. Perhaps the Philosopher is innocent. But you I think are not!" insinuated Cyril as he marched out of the Prefect's office.

Month after month Orestes struggled to keep the peace in Alexandria as Cyril continued his uncle's religious wars against all who opposed his radical orthodox Christianity. Month after month Cyril challenged his secular authority, demanding that his rule as patriarch ranked above Orestes' own. It was a political war being fought in the streets with the innocent paying the price in their daily lives. Orestes on his part continued to see Hypatia's wise council which she readily gave as the most prominent intellectual in Alexandria and as he perpetual teacher. Finally, Orestes acted openly against Cyril's constant disruption of civil order when he ordered the torture of one of Cyril's men for instigating a riot at a Jewish gathering held at the theatre. Cyril offered Orestes a precious copy of the Bible as a token of his willing to forgive the prefect. Orestes rejected it, mindful that accepting the Bible would signal to the province that he condoned Cyril's actions.

"Did you hear?" asked a young man as Orestes left the Caesareum. "Orestes rejected the patriarch's gift!"

"Heresy!" shouted another. "He is no Christian!"

"He is bewitched!" called another. "Hypatia has bewitched him!"

"He must pay for consorting with witches!" cried a Nitrian monk. Picking up stones from the ground he hurled them in Orestes' direction.

"Pay he shall!" yelled Brother Ammonius as he threw a stone at Orestes. Blood gushed from Orestes head and face. Ammonius continued to throw stones until it looked like Orestes no long had a face at all. Horrified a young woman helped Orestes escape Ammonius' assault as he headed for the home of his beloved Philosopher.

"Lysimachus, fetch the doctor," commanded Hypatia as she helped Orestes lay down. As her slave obeyed, Hypatia carefully applied a heavy wool rag upon his cheek and forehead to stop the bleeding. "You are going to be fine, Orestes. I know it."

"As long as they don't hurt you," declared Orestes weakly.

"That is in God's hands. I will not let Cyril's Nitrian monks or the parabalanoi or any other so-called Christian interfere with my work. I am as I always was. I will change. The agents of hatred will not rule my life."

"Even if they kill you?"

"I would rather die tomorrow true to myself and to what I believe in than live one hundred years in a lie. These people do not uphold the teachings of Jesus. It is all about power and control and hate. Hate for anyone and anything that contradicts the interests of those in power. If I am martyred, then I am martyred. Better a dead servant of love and peace than a living soldier of hate."

"You never cease to inspire me, Hypatia."

"I am not the Light, Orestes, only a candle for the Light."

"Hypatia the Philosopher is a witch, I tell you! A witch!" yelled Peter, lector of the Caesareum. Two parishioners carried a basket into the street filled with books. Peter picked one up and raised it above his head, "Here is the proof! Books on mathematics! Geometry! Astrological charts showing the positions of the wanderers. It's the devil's work! Divination and magic! And yet you honour her? Call her 'my lady' and listen to her? Even our Prefect listens to her like the pagan lapdog we know he really is. Either she has bewitched him or he was never a true Christian in the first place. And then there is poor Ammonius. Martyred by prefect.

What did he do but throw a few stones in the prefect's direction? It is unfair, I tell you! Unjust! Look! Look! There she is! Hypatia!"

Turning around, the mob spotted Hypatia as she drove her chariot nearby. Peter seized the reins of her horse. Hypatia looked him in the eye, "I forgive you."

Epilogue

"…and dragging her from her carriage, they took her to the church called Cæsareum, where they completely stripped her, and then murdered her with tiles. After tearing her body in pieces, they took her mangled limbs to a place called Cinaron, and there burnt them. This affair brought not the least opprobrium, not only upon Cyril, but also upon the whole Alexandrian church. And surely nothing can be farther from the spirit of Christianity than the allowance of massacres, fights, and transactions of that sort. This happened in the month of March during Lent, in the fourth year of Cyril's episcopate, under the tenth consulate of Honorius, and the sixth of Theodosius," read Hildegarde.

"What about Orestes?" asked the novice.

"He was never seen in Alexandria again. Many believe he was murdered after the mob burnt Hypatia's books in the agora. Shortly thereafter Cyril completed the final expulsion of all the Jews from Alexandria. For these acts and many others, the church rewarded him by making him a saint, though not giving him a feast day.

"Hypatia's murder had a chilling effect on intellectual life in Alexandria. Though it did not immediately end advanced learning in the city, Cyril's increase in power and authority sent a clear message that anyone who challenged the teachings of the Church, no matter how unintentionally, could expect the same fate.

"What about Bede? Does this mean his books are worthless?"

"Bede was first and foremost a monk," explained Prioress Hildegard. "His loyalties were first to mother Church. For all must submit to the rulings of our church leaders and profess agreement with them, no matter if they are right or wrong. To fail to do so is to risk being burned as a heretic. Who will risk that when it is far easier to obey the Holy Father in Rome? And yet … I cannot obey. The visions God gives me supersedes everything. Popes, bishops, archbishops are all men! I do not know yet what the answer is to the problem, but this I do know: I will find the answer!"

Latitude and Longitude Coordinates for Select Cities in the Roman Empire

(North to South)

Mamucium (Manchester): 53.4808° N, 2.2426° W

Camulodunum (Caer Colun; Colchester): 51.88921, 0.90421

Londinium (London): 51.5074° N, 0.1278° W

Colonia Claudia Ara Agrippinensium (Köln; Cologne): 50.9375° N, 6.9603° E

Lutetia Parisiorum (Paris): 48.8566° N, 2.3522° E

Mediolanum (Milan): 45.4642° N, 9.1900° E

Roma (Rome): 41.9028° N, 12.4964° E

Constantinopoli (Constaniople): 41.0082° N, 28.9784° E

Αθήνα (Athens): 37.9838° N, 23.7275° E

ושומרון (Samaria): 32.4229° N, 35.3027° E

ירושלים (Jerusalem): 31.7683° N, 35.2137° E

Αλεξάνδρεια (Alexandria): 31.2001° N, 29.9187° E

Timeline

2136 BCE; Chinese astronomers record first known record of an eclipse.

1300 BCE; Shang Dynasty Chinese begin recording solar and lunar eclipses. First known observation of a supernova is recorded on an oracle bone of tortoise.

700 BCE; birth of Greek poet Hesiod, author of "Theogony" which tells the creation story of the gods, of man, and of the separate creation of woman.

c. 300 BCE; Chinese astronomer Shi Shen catalogues 809 stars in 122 constellations and makes the first records of sun spots.

330 BCE; Alexander the Great founds the city of Alexandria in Egypt.

327 BCE; Epicurus begins challenging Hesiod's "Theogony" through philosophy. Founds the prominent Epicurean school that establishes the first theories on the nature of matter.

323 BCE; death of Alexander the Great. Alexander's general Ptolemy Soter takes over control of Egypt as its governor.

320 BCE; Governor Ptolemy Soter sets up his capital in Alexandria.

c. 310 BCE; birth of astronomer Aristarchus.

305 BCE; Governor Ptolemy Soter proclaims himself Pharaoh. Creation of the Ptolemaic dynasty.

c. 305 BCE; Pharaoh Ptolemy I creates the cult of Serapis to unify Greeks and Egyptians together under one religion with worship integrating beliefs and imagery from both cultures.

c. 295 BCE; exiled Athenian Governor Demetrius of Phalerum organizes construction of the "Temple of the Muses" (Musaeum) complex as a library and centre of intellectual discourse and learning. The library's collections grow so large that two sister libraries are built to house more books and provide more classrooms to educators.

287 BCE; first sacking of Rome by the Senones, a tribe from the Aedui Confederation.

285 BCE; death of Pharaoh Ptolemy I. Ptolemy II ascends as Pharaoh.

240 BCE; Chinese astronomers record the first appearance of Halley's Comet.

217 BCE, 17th December; first recorded public Saturnalia banquets.

c. 210 BCE; death of astronomer Aristarchus.

190 BCE; birth of astronomer Hipparchus of Nicaea.

120 BCE; death of astronomer Hipparchus of Nicaea.

70 BCE; birth of Cleopatra to Pharaoh Ptolemy XII Auletes

30 BCE; completion of the Caesareum in Alexandria.

50 BCE; Lucretius publishes *De Rerum Natura* which explores and clarifies the teachings of Greek philosopher Epicurus and lays the philosophical foundation for many sciences.

4 BCE; Chinese record a rare hypernova in the constellation Aquila.

52 CE; Apostle Paul writes his letters to Thessalonica (Therma) in Macedonia.

c. 57 CE; Apostle Paul writes his letters to the church in the cosmopolitan city Corinth, and his letter to the church in Galatia in Asia Minor.

62 CE; Apostle Paul writes his letter to the church in the Roman provincial capital city of Ephesus, to the church in the Macedonian city of Philippi, and to his friend Philemon, the bishop of Collose.

c. 65 CE; Apostle Paul writes his letters to his missionary friends Timothy and Titus.

100 CE; birth of Christian apologist, Saint Justin (Martyr) in Samaria.

165 CE; Saint Justin is beheaded and martyred.

185 CE; astronomers in China observe SN185 as it goes supernova, calling it a "guest star."

200 CE; completion of the Mishnah which puts into writing the "oral Torah."

272 CE; Flavia Iulia Helena Augusta gives birth to Flavius Valerius Aurelius Constantinus Augustus, later known as Constantine.

325 CE; Emperor Constantine calls the First Council of Nicaea at which the Nicaean Creed is drafted.

330 CE; Emperor Constantine founds the city of Constantinople in modern day Turkey.

335 CE; Church of the Holy Sepulchre consecrated in Jerusalem.

337 CE; death of Constantine in Constantinople.

354 CE, 25th December; Christmas is celebrated for the first time in Rome as a Christian celebration of the birth of Jesus Christ.

c. 355 CE; Hypatia born to Greek mathematician Theon of Alexandria.

370 CE; birth of Synesius of Cyrene.

379 CE; Theodosius I becomes emperor of the Roman Empire. Ruling from Constantinople, he becomes the last emperor to rule a united Roman Empire.

380 CE, 27th February; Theodosius I issues the Edict of Thessalonica declaring Nicene Trinitarian Christianity as the only legitimate religion of the empire. All other (Christian) philosophies and/or interpretations of the Bible become heretical.

385 CE; Theophilus becomes Patriarch of Alexandria.

390 CE; Synesius arrives in Alexandria. He quickly becomes Hypatia's most famous student after studying with her for five years.

391 CE; the Caesareum and the Temple of Serapis are destroyed and then converted into Christian churches. Theophilus orders the destruction of the temples' libraries, both branch libraries to the Great Library. Destruction of all "pagan" temples, religious sites, and sacred objects.

393 CE; Theodosius I bans all "pagan" rituals at the Olympic games. Dissolution of the Vestal Virgins in Rome.

395 CE, January; death of Emperor Theodosius I. Synesius leaves Alexandria.

405 CE; death of Theon of Alexandria. Orestes is baptized into Christianity by Atticus of Constantinople.

409 CE; Synesius is chosen as Bishop of Ptolemais. Married and with three sons, he accepts but refuses to leave his family.

410 CE; the Goths sack Rome for three days.

c. 410 CE; Orestes is appointed Praefectus augustalis (provincial governor) of the Diocese of Egypt.

412 CE; death of Theophilus. Elevation of his nephew Cyril as Patriarch. Cyril makes the Caesareum his headquarters.

413 CE; death of Synesius of Cyrene.

415 CE March; Hypatia murdered by Christian zealots in the Caesareum.

725 CE; Bede, an Anglo-Saxon monk from Northumbria publishes *De temporum ratione* (The Reckoning of Time).

1006 30 April – 1 May CE; SN 1006 becomes the first globally observed supernova with observations across Europe, Asia, and the Americas.

c. 1530 CE; Polish astronomer Nicolaus Copernicus finishes *De Revolutionibus Orbium Coelestium* (On the Revolutions of the Celestial Spheres) to resurrect heliocentrism.

1596 CE; Johann Kepler publishes *Mysterium Cosmographicum* supporting Copernican heliocentrism and asserting elliptical orbits around the sun in contradiction to Ptolemy.

5 July 1687 CE; Isaac Newton publishes *Philosophiæ Naturalis Principia Mathematica* containing his three laws

of planetary motion and presenting his case for universal gravity.

Bibliography

Hypatia of Alexandria

Agora: the "Reel" vs. the "Real" Hypatia

https://faithljustice.wordpress.com/2010/06/01/agora-hypatia-part-i/

https://faithljustice.wordpress.com/2010/06/03/agora-hypatia-part-ii/

https://faithljustice.wordpress.com/2010/06/08/agora-hypatia-part-iii/

Hypatia: Pagan philosopher, scientist, mathematician, and civic leader

http://www.suppressedhistories.net/secrethistory/hypatia.html

Hypatia

http://www.math.wichita.edu/history/women/hypatia.html

Hypatia: Mathematician and Astronomer

https://www.britannica.com/biography/Hypatia

Badass women of science: Hypatia of Alexandria

https://violentmetaphors.com/2013/06/04/hypatia/

Chicago University: Hypatia

http://penelope.uchicago.edu/~grout/encyclopaedia_romana/greece/paganism/hypatia.html

Hypatia of Alexandria

http://www-history.mcs.st-and.ac.uk/Biographies/Hypatia.html

Hypatia

http://hypatia.ucsd.edu/~kl/hypatia.html

Ten Great Female Philosophers: the Thinking Woman's Women

http://www.independent.co.uk/news/uk/this-britain/ten-great-female-philosophers-the-thinking-womans-women-299061.html

Hypatia of Alexandria: The Passing of Philosophy to Religion

http://www.ancient.eu/article/76/

Hellenistic Egypt

Britannica: Serapis

https://www.britannica.com/topic/Serapis

What happened to the Great Library at Alexandria?

http://www.ancient.eu/article/207/

The Burning of the Library of Alexandria

https://ehistory.osu.edu/articles/burning-library-alexandria

The Mysterious Fate of the Great Library of Alexandria

http://jameshannam.com/library.htm

The Great Library of Alexandria

http://penelope.uchicago.edu/~grout/encyclopaedia_romana/greece/paganism/library.html

The Library of the Serapeum

http://penelope.uchicago.edu/~grout/encyclopaedia_romana/greece/paganism/daughter.html

Sacred Destinations: the Serapeum

http://www.sacred-destinations.com/egypt/alexandria-serapeum

The Caesareum of Alexandria: Scene of Crime

http://www.cosmographica.com/spaceart/alexandria/caesareum.html

It's All Greek To Me – The Complicated Story of Hanukkah

http://blogs.timesofisrael.com/its-all-greek-to-me-the-complicated-story-of-hanukkah/

Hanukkah Part I, The Ptolemaic Empire

https://youtu.be/54flSoFxKI0

Ptolemy I Soter: Macedonian King of Egypt

https://www.britannica.com/biography/Ptolemy-I-Soter

Ptolemy II Philadelphus: Macdoniam King of Egypt

https://www.britannica.com/biography/Ptolemy-II-Philadelphus

History.com: Cleopatra

http://www.history.com/topics/ancient-history/cleopatra

Greek Spirituality and Mythology

Greek Mythology Gods and Goddesses Documentary

https://youtu.be/-MSEsh6jgHE

Eileithyia

http://www.theoi.com/Ouranios/Eileithyia.html

Prometheus

http://www.theoi.com/Titan/TitanPrometheus.html

Britannica: Hesiod

https://www.britannica.com/biography/Hesiod

Hesiod: Theogony (full text)

http://chs.harvard.edu/CHS/article/display/5289

Pandora

http://www.theoi.com/Heroine/Pandora.html

The Earth Mother Rules

http://manicscribbler.blogspot.co.uk/2017/06/the-earth-mother-rules-guest-author.html

Britannica: Serapis

https://www.britannica.com/topic/Serapis

Greek History, Language, and Geography

Greece: Secrets of the Past

http://www.historymuseum.ca/cmc/exhibitions/civil/greece/gr0000e.shtml

Greece: Daily Life

http://www.historymuseum.ca/cmc/exhibitions/civil/greece/gr1150e.shtml

Greece: Alphabets and Writing

http://www.historymuseum.ca/cmc/exhibitions/civil/greece/gr1060e.shtml

How to Address Your Teacher

https://harzing.com/publications/white-papers/how-to-address-your-teacher

Ancient Greek Names

https://tekeli.li/onomastikon/Ancient-World/Greece/Male.html

How to be polite in Greek

https://blogs.transparent.com/greek/how-to-be-polite-in-greek/

Behind the Name: Hypatia

https://www.behindthename.com/name/hypatia

Acropolis Hill

http://www.greeka.com/attica/athens/athens-excursions/acropolis.htm

Ancient Greek Female Names

http://monsaventinus.wikia.com/wiki/Ancient_Greek_Female_Names_(Greek_Community)

Athens Geography

http://www.greeka.com/attica/athens/athens-geography.htm

Socratic Method

https://www.law.uchicago.edu/socratic-method

Critical Thinking Community: Socratic Method

http://www.criticalthinking.org/pages/socratic-teaching/606

Greek Philosophy, Science, and Mathematics

Greek Mathematics

https://www.youtube.com/watch?v=UPlqJaUi5jE (part one)

https://www.youtube.com/watch?v=56Yy1odPLag (part two)

Plato's Republic: A Utopia for the Individual

https://philosophynow.org/issues/70/Platos_Republic_A_Utopia_For_The_Individual

Democritus: Greek Philosopher

https://www.britannica.com/biography/Democritus

The Nature of Women in Plato and Aristotle

https://www.classicsnetwork.com/essays/the-nature-of-women-in-plato-and/786

Epicurus: Greek Philosopher

https://www.britannica.com/biography/Epicurus

How Greek Maths Changes the World

https://youtu.be/F97UvxQWqrk

Who was Plato?

http://quatr.us/greeks/philosophy/plato.htm

Ancient History: Greek Astronomy

http://www.ancient.eu/Greek_Astronomy/

Hipparchus of Nicea

http://www.ancient.eu/Hipparchus_of_Nicea/

Aristarchus of Samos

http://www.ancient.eu/Aristarchus_of_Samos/

Aristotle. *Politics.* Translated by Benjamin Jowett. New York: Dover Publications, 2000.

Jewish History, Culture, and Beliefs

Ancient Jewish History: Pharisees, Sadducees & Essenes http://www.jewishvirtuallibrary.org/pharisees-sadducees-and-essenes

Why is Jewishness Passed Down Through the Mother?

http://www.chabad.org/theJewishWoman/article_cdo/aid/968282/jewish/Why-Is-Jewishness-Passed-Down-Through-the-Mother.htm

The Jewish Temples: After the Babylonian Exile

http://www.jewishvirtuallibrary.org/after-the-babylonian-exile

The History of the Talmud

http://www.simpletoremember.com/articles/a/talmud-history/

Reform Judaism: the Talmud

http://reformjudaism.org/talmud

The Talmud's Deep Misogyny: No Women Allowed

http://www.tabletmag.com/jewish-life-and-religion/195125/daf-yomi-147

The Role of Women

http://www.jewfaq.org/women.htm

Passover Cleaning Checklist

http://www.chabad.org/holidays/passover/pesach_cdo/aid/117150/jewish/Cleaning-Checklist.htm

What is Chametz?

http://www.chabad.org/holidays/passover/pesach_cdo/aid/1742/jewish/What-Is-Chametz.htm

Real Simple: Preparing for the Passover Meal Checklist

https://www.realsimple.com/holidays-entertaining/holidays/more-holidays/seder-meal

Tori Avey: What is Hanukkah?

https://toriavey.com/hanukkah-the-festival-of-lights/

Temple Israel Hanukkah Service

https://templeisrael.com/pdfs/hanukkah%20service.pdf

Chanukah (Hanukkah) Guide

http://www.chabad.org/holidays/chanukah/article_cdo/aid/603798/jewish/Chanukah-Guide.htm

Roman Culture and History

The Deception of Constantine

https://youtu.be/TY1_sYnr0gE

Orestes

https://www.revolvy.com/main/index.php?s=Orestes%20(prefect)

Lucretius (c. 99 BCE to c 55 BCE)

http://www.iep.utm.edu/lucretiu/

Lucretius: Latin Poet and Philosopher

https://www.britannica.com/biography/Lucretius

Roman Timeline 4th Century AD

http://www.unrv.com/empire/timeline-4th-century.php

On the Nature of Things

http://classics.mit.edu/Carus/nature_things.html

Thessalonica

http://www.ancient.eu/Thessalonica/

Did the Romans Invent Christmas?

http://www.historytoday.com/matt-salusbury/did-romans-invent-christmas

Saturnalia

http://penelope.uchicago.edu/~grout/encyclopaedia_romana/calendar/saturnalia.html

Saturnalia

http://www.ancient.eu/Saturnalia/

Duducu, Jem. *The Romans in 100 Facts.* Stroud: Amberley Publishing, 2015.

Rockefeller, Laurel A. *Boudicca, Britain's Queen of the Iceni.* Pennsylvania: Laurel A. Rockefeller Books, 2014.

Christians and Christianity

Socrates (of Constantinople): Church historian

https://www.ccel.org/ccel/socrates

(Cyril) The Villain Who Gave Us "Mother of God"

http://www.thedailybeast.com/the-villain-who-gave-us-mother-of-god

Tyndale Archive: the Letters of Paul

http://tyndalearchive.com/scriptures/www.innvista.co m/scriptures/compare/letters.htm

The Church at Corinth

https://www.bibleodyssey.org/en/places/related-articles/church-at-corinth

The Fathers of the Church

http://www.newadvent.org/fathers/index.html

Justin Martyr: Defender of the "True Philosophy"

http://www.christianitytoday.com/history/people/evan gelistsandapologists/justin-martyr.html

Justin Martyr: Hortatory Address to the Greeks

http://www.newadvent.org/fathers/0129.htm

God's Word to Women: Did Paul Really Say, "Let the Women Keep Silent in the Churches"?

https://godswordtowomen.org/Preato2.htm

New Advent: Synesius of Cyrene

http://www.newadvent.org/cathen/14386a.htm

The texts of Synesius

http://www.livius.org/articles/person/synesius-of-cyrene/synesius-texts/

Synesius of Cyrene

http://www.livius.org/articles/person/synesius-of-cyrene/

New World Encyclopedia: Cyril of Alexandria

http://www.newworldencyclopedia.org/entry/Cyril_of_Alexandria

St. Theophilus of Alexandria

http://www.catholic.org/saints/saint.php?saint_id=826

Socrates Scholasticus. *Nicene and Post-Nicene Fathers,* ed. Philip Schaff. (Grand Rapids, MI: Christian Classics Ethereal Library, 2009), 403.

Astronomy

Understanding Astronomy: Motion of the Stars

http://physics.weber.edu/schroeder/ua/starmotion.html

Your Sky custom star maps for your location

http://www.fourmilab.ch/cgi-bin/Yoursky

University Lowbrow Astronomers Naked Eye Observer's Guide

https://www.umich.edu/~lowbrows/guide/eye.html

Ursa Major Constellation

http://www.constellation-guide.com/constellation-list/ursa-major-constellation/

Ursa Minor Constellation

http://www.constellation-guide.com/constellation-list/ursa-minor-constellation/

Ursa Minor

http://www.astro.wisc.edu/~dolan/constellations/constellations/Ursa_Minor.html

Stellar Death

http://www.novacelestia.com/space_art_stars/stellar_death.html

2,000-Year-Old Supernova Mystery Solved By NASA Telescopes. https://www.space.com/13374-ancient-supernova-mystery-solved.html

Ancient History: Greek Astronomy

http://www.ancient.eu/Greek_Astronomy/

How fast will the sun become a red giant?

https://physics.stackexchange.com/questions/25622/how-fast-will-the-sun-become-a-red-giant

Supernova SN 1006: Cause of brightest stellar event in recorded history illuminated

https://www.sciencedaily.com/releases/2012/09/120927091538.htm

What did Isaac Newton Discover?

https://www.universetoday.com/38643/what-did-isaac-newton-discover/

Johannes Kepler Biography

https://www.space.com/15787-johannes-kepler.html

The Quadrant and the Sextant

http://www.sites.hps.cam.ac.uk/starry/quadrant.html

Other resources

Hebrew Names for Girls

https://www.thoughtco.com/hebrew-names-for-girls-2076845

Hebrew Endearments

https://forum.wordreference.com/threads/hebrew-endearments.347296/

Roman Dress

http://www.roman-empire.net/society/soc-dress.html

About This Series

The Legendary Women of World History Series was first created in March 2014 in response to poor performance to a simple survey question asking people to name five women from across history whose lives still touch ours today. When less than 10% of the 50-100 people surveyed could name just five and less than 5% could name ten, author and historian Laurel A. Rockefeller decided to take action. The result was this author's best-selling narrative biography, "Boudicca, Britain's Queen of the Iceni" which came to audiences in audio edition in September of the same year.

In May 2015 work began on adapting the Legendary Women of World History Series into a stage drama series. The goal of the Legendary Women of World History Drama Series is both educational and entertainment, bringing the compelling stories of inspiring women to audiences while simultaneously offering commanding lead roles to actresses and offering educational settings enhanced opportunities working with the challenges of period dramas.

Today you can find the Legendary Women of World History Series and Legendary Women of World History

Drama Series in English, French, Spanish, Chinese, Italian, Portuguese, German, and Welsh with more languages being offered as series popularity grows. It is the goal of this series to improve global history literacy while inspiring women and men with a more accurate understanding of history. It is the hope of this author and historian that the stage dramas will also help address inequities in the entertainment industry which so far have offered limited opportunities for women, people of colour, and religious minorities.

Thank you for reading this narrative biography. It is my fondest wish you will explore more of the Legendary Women of World History and be inspired!

Share the love of this book and the Legendary Women of World History Series by kindly reviewing this book on your blog, website, and on major retailer websites. Your review not only offers this author your feedback for improvement of this book series, but helps other people find this book so they can enjoy it as well. Only a few sentences and a few minutes of your time is all it takes to share the love with those who want to enjoy it too.

Made in the USA
Las Vegas, NV
25 October 2024

10432617R00059